D0862469

Week-by-Week
MATH REVIEW
for the Digital Classroom

Ready-to-Use, Animated PowerPoint® Slideshows With Practice Pages That Help Students Master Key Math Skills and Concepts

by Steve Wyborney

New York ○ Toronto ○ London ○ Auckland ○ Sydney
New Delhi ○ Mexico City ○ Hong Kong ○ Buenos Aires

Teaching Resources

Dedication

For Ed and Julie Dashiell, from "your son"

Editor: Maria L. Chang
Cover design by Michelle Kim
Interior design by Robert Dominguez

ISBN: 978-0-545-77343-0
Copyright © 2015 by Steve Wyborney
All rights reserved.
Printed in the U.S.A.

1 2 3 4 5 6 7 8 9 10   40   20 19 18 17 16 15

Table of Contents

Table of Contents

Introduction

Welcome to *Week-by-Week Math Review for the Digital Classroom*!

Mathematical instruction can be a complex mixture of gaining new knowledge and skills while continually growing conceptual understanding, strengthening foundations, and developing rich, insightful connections among ideas. Our most powerful moments of growth come when we encounter content, discover new pathways, and think carefully about our ideas from multiple perspectives.

Encountering content is critical, and there is great power in repeatedly reviewing that content over time. *Week-by-Week Math Review for the Digital Classroom* is designed to help you and your students encounter rich mathematical content in meaningful ways as you travel through the school year.

This unique and highly flexible resource combines 35 ready-to-use PowerPoint® review lessons (on the enclosed CD) with reproducible, leveled practice sheets. The lessons place you, the classroom teacher, squarely at the center of the resource, and I am certain you will sense your focal role in this resource as soon as you begin using it. This format empowers you during the instructional sequence by providing visual prompts, meaningful animations, high-quality questions, and response/feedback opportunities that are completely paced by you.

The purposeful animation in the lessons is designed to make the math concepts completely accessible to students—possibly in ways that they have never seen before. I fully recognize that animation can provide either clarity or distraction, and I have developed each lesson with great care to ensure that the animation will work to simplify and illuminate mathematical concepts that students might otherwise find difficult to understand.

Thank you for including *Week-by-Week Math Review for the Digital Classroom* among your resources. I know that the resources we all treasure are the ones that make our lives simpler and our students' learning clearer. That is exactly what I believe this resource will do for you.

Kind regards,
Steve Wyborney

How to Use This Book

Lesson Components

Week-by-Week Math Review for the Digital Classroom includes two key components: the animated PowerPoint lessons on CD and the reproducible student response pages. The animated lessons are very simple to use and are intended to be taught before using the response pages.

Each lesson features four mathematical concepts that support today's higher standards. The review lessons have been designed so that a concept that appears for the first time in a given lesson will appear again in the lessons that follow, both in the animated slideshow as well as on the accompanying student response pages. Each time the concept reappears, the challenge level will increase. The table of contents lists the math concepts and skills in each week's lesson.

To begin teaching an animated lesson, simply launch the chosen PowerPoint file. (For whole-class instruction, connect your computer to the interactive whiteboard or to a projector in front of a blank screen.) You will quickly find that the lesson is designed purposefully with click-by-click animations and scripting. The scripting will appear on the bottom of the screen and is carefully calculated to match the timing and pacing of the lesson.

The script is a guide and is intended as an option, if you choose to use it. Some of your most powerful teaching moments may come when you follow the script to a point where you discover a prime instructional opportunity that is not in the script—the kind of opportunity that you, the classroom teacher, are well aware of because you understand the precise, specific needs of your students. When you find those moments, pursue them, and then return to the lesson when the time is right.

As mentioned earlier, each lesson includes multiple concepts. At the end of each concept section, you will find a series of "lightning round" questions. Generally these slides contain no script. Instead, a single click typically leads to a question, and the next click reveals the answer. You will likely feel the pace change at the end of each section during the lightning round.

The second component in this resource—the reproducible response pages—is designed to give students the opportunity to practice the skills and concepts presented in the lesson. Each page contains multiple concepts that match the sequence, form, and style of the animated lesson they have just reviewed. The response pages are leveled so that you can adapt them to student needs. You may choose to use the simpler page, the more challenging page, or a combination of the two, depending on the abilities of your students. The pages can be used independently, with partners, in small groups, or with the whole class.

Planning and Sequencing Options

The series-review design offers multiple sequencing options. You may choose to do the lessons in the order in which they are presented, beginning with Week 1 and proceeding through Week 35. Each lesson will review prior concepts and introduce one new concept. The lessons have been carefully sequenced to build upon one another so that you can teach them in the order provided.

You may also choose to select lessons—or even portions of lessons—in any order to best suit instruction.

An additional option is to cycle through lesson sets so that the content in each lesson is entirely different than the content of the prior lesson, and the lessons are taught without reviewing prior content. If you choose to use this approach, here is a guide that will be helpful. Remember that each lesson contains multiple concepts. A table is provided below to detail the lesson numbers in this cycle.

Cycle 1 ➡	1	5	9	13	17	21	25	29	33
Cycle 2 ➡	2	6	10	14	18	22	26	30	34
Cycle 3 ➡	3	7	11	15	19	23	27	31	35
Cycle 4 ➡	4	8	12	16	20	24	28	32	

Instructional Options

While the book has been written to facilitate whole-class instruction, there are a wide variety of possible uses for the combination of animated lessons and student response pages, including:

- small-group lessons
- independent lessons
- student-led lessons (with the support of the displayed lesson script)
- professional development

Take advantage of opportunities in which students teach the lesson. The script will be there to support them, and you will be amazed at the questions that they begin to ask of one another as they encounter content together.

The Teacher's Role

Each lesson has been purposefully designed to connect students to the content through the teacher. This is not a digital resource that minimizes the role of the teacher. In contrast, the instruction runs directly through you, as it should. No one knows your students better than you. Although each lesson is complete and can be taught as listed, I strongly believe that some of the best instructional experiences will happen when you pause the lesson and pursue a question or opportunity that has been revealed. In the moments when you say, "That's an interesting question. What do you think?" or "Can you explain your thinking?" or "What is another way to think about this?" you will find excellent opportunities to guide your students toward successful and powerful mathematical learning.

Name _____ Date _____

Write the product.

30 x 7 =	**50 x 3 =**	**20 x 30 =**

What is the volume?

 = 1 cubic unit

          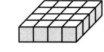

_____ cubic units   _____ cubic units   _____ cubic units

Write each decimal in expanded form.

52.76	**4.293**	**819.6**

Write two statements that compare each product to its factors.
The first one has been started for you.

7 x 5 = 35	**6 x 8 = 48**	**7 x 19 = 133**

35 is _____ times

greater than _____.

35 is _____ times

greater than _____.

Week-by-Week Math Review for the Digital Classroom: Grade 5 © 2015 by Steve Wyborney, Scholastic Teaching Resources

Name _____ **Date** _____

Write the product.

90 × 60 =	**80 × 500 =**	**7 × 8,000 =**	**400 × 600 =**

What is the volume?

 = 1 cubic unit

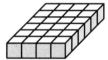    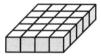

_____ cubic units   _____ cubic units   _____ cubic units   _____ cubic units

Write each decimal in expanded form.

52.916	**385.42**	**16.174**	**915.58**

Write two statements that compare each product to its factors.
The first one has been started for you.

9 × 14 = 126	**22 × 5 = 110**	**12 × 50 = 600**	**25 × 32 = 800**
126 is _____ times greater than _____.			
126 is _____ times greater than _____.			

Name _____ Date _____

What is the volume?

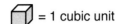 = 1 cubic unit

_____ cubic units   _____ cubic units   _____ cubic units

Write each decimal in expanded form.

9.286   **78.54**   **394.72**

Write two statements that compare each product to its factors.
The first one has been started for you.

5 x 9 = 45   **4 x 25 = 100**   **20 x 7 = 140**

45 is _____ times

greater than _____.

45 is _____ times

greater than _____.

Find the missing numerator or denominator.

$$\frac{7}{10} = \frac{}{30}$$ $$\frac{4}{7} = \frac{24}{}$$ $$\frac{35}{} = \frac{5}{7}$$

Week-by-Week Math Review for the Digital Classroom: Grade 5 © 2015 by Steve Wyborney, Scholastic Teaching Resources

Name _____ **Date** _____

What is the volume?

 = 1 cubic unit

 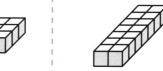 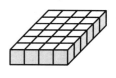

_____ cubic units | _____ cubic units | _____ cubic units | _____ cubic units

---

Write each decimal in expanded form.

52.938 | **17.688** | **2,569.7** | **482.659**

Write two statements that compare each product to its factors.
The first one has been started for you.

17 × 14 = 238 | **3 × 297 = 891** | **55 × 38 = 2,090** | **286 × 4 = 1,144**

238 is _____ times

greater than _____.

238 is _____ times

greater than _____.

Find the missing numerator or denominator.

$\dfrac{5}{8} = \dfrac{\quad}{32}$ | $\dfrac{3}{8} = \dfrac{27}{\quad}$ | $\dfrac{30}{\quad} = \dfrac{6}{11}$ | $\dfrac{\quad}{3} = \dfrac{16}{24}$

Week-by-Week Math Review for the Digital Classroom: Grade 5 © 2015 by Steve Wyborney, Scholastic Teaching Resources

Name _____ Date _____

Write each decimal in expanded form.

6.254 | 38.29 | 186.47

Write two statements that compare each product to its factors.
The first one has been started for you.

90 × 3 = 270 | **15 × 12 = 180** | **36 × 24 = 864**

270 is _____ times

greater than _____.

270 is _____ times

greater than _____.

Find the missing numerator or denominator.

$\dfrac{}{45} = \dfrac{3}{5}$ | $\dfrac{2}{3} = \dfrac{14}{}$ | $\dfrac{7}{} = \dfrac{28}{36}$

Evaluate each expression.

$3 \times (5 - 1) =$ | $(12 + 6) \div (2 + 1) =$ | $(50 - 1) \div 7 =$

Week-by-Week Math Review for the Digital Classroom: Grade 5 © 2015 by Steve Wyborney, Scholastic Teaching Resources

Name _____ **Date** _____

Write each decimal in expanded form.

28.671	985.64	2,358.26	59.737

Write two statements that compare each product to its factors.
The first one has been started for you.

50 × 70 = 3,500	26 × 39 = 1,014	83 × 67 = 5,561	7 × 549 = 3,843

3,500 is _____ times

greater than _____.

3,500 is _____ times

greater than _____.

Find the missing numerator or denominator.

$$\frac{}{63} = \frac{8}{9} \qquad \frac{10}{17} = \frac{30}{} \qquad \frac{7}{} = \frac{56}{72} \qquad \frac{32}{} = \frac{4}{7}$$

Evaluate each expression.

$(62 - 6) \div (2 \times 4) =$	$(3 \times 8) \div (9 - 3) =$	$8 \times (7 + 8) =$	$(27 + 15) \div 6 =$

Name _____ **Date** _____

Write two statements that compare each product to its factors.
The first one has been started for you.

| **8 × 15 = 120** | **25 × 40 = 1,000** | **22 × 15 = 330** |

120 is _____ times

greater than _____.

120 is _____ times

greater than _____.

Find the missing numerator or denominator.

$$\frac{15}{24} = \frac{5}{\rule{1cm}{0.4pt}}$$

$$\frac{\rule{1cm}{0.4pt}}{36} = \frac{5}{9}$$

$$\frac{7}{8} = \frac{\rule{1cm}{0.4pt}}{32}$$

Evaluate each expression.

| **8 × (4 + 2) =** | **(40 − 5) ÷ (2 + 5) =** | **(4 × 9) ÷ 6 =** |

How many times greater or smaller is the second number compared to the first?

| **40** | **3,000** | **70** |
| **4,000** | **3** | **0.07** |

100 times greater
_____   _____   _____

Week-by-Week Math Review for the Digital Classroom: Grade 5 © 2015 by Steve Wyborney, Scholastic Teaching Resources

Name _____ **Date** _____

Write two statements that compare each product to its factors.
The first one has been started for you.

26 × 38 = 988	9 × 425 = 3,825	17 × 13 = 221	68 × 45 = 3,060
988 is _____ times greater than _____. 988 is _____ times greater than _____.			

Find the missing numerator or denominator.

$$\frac{36}{81} = \frac{4}{}$$ $$\frac{}{56} = \frac{6}{7}$$ $$\frac{6}{9} = \frac{}{63}$$ $$\frac{7}{} = \frac{49}{56}$$

Evaluate each expression.

9 × (9 + 9) =   (42 ÷ 7) ÷ (12 ÷ 2) =   (8 + 8) ÷ 8 =   (7 × 7) + (15 − 14) =

How many times greater or smaller is the second number compared to the first?

700,000	90	0.02	800,000
700	0.09	200	8

| ____ | ____ | ____ | ____ |

Name _____ Date _____

Find the missing numerator or denominator.

$$\frac{2}{5} = \frac{}{45}$$ $$\frac{4}{7} = \frac{32}{}$$ $$\frac{24}{} = \frac{6}{7}$$

Evaluate each expression.

$$54 \div (5 + 4) =$$ $$(36 \div 4) \times (5 + 3) =$$ $$7 + (9 \times 4) =$$

How many times greater or smaller is the second number compared to the first?

20	0.001	50
0.2	1	0.5

_____   _____   _____

What is the volume?

 = 1 cubic unit

_____ cubic units   _____ cubic units   _____ cubic units

Week-by-Week Math Review for the Digital Classroom: Grade 5 © 2015 by Steve Wyborney, Scholastic Teaching Resources

Name _____ **Date** _____

Find the missing numerator or denominator.

$$\frac{7}{3} = \frac{}{18}$$ $$\frac{8}{9} = \frac{48}{}$$ $$\frac{50}{} = \frac{5}{9}$$ $$\frac{}{8} = \frac{21}{56}$$

Evaluate each expression.

72 ÷ (24 ÷ 3) = | **(15 ÷ 5) × (7 + 7) =** | **100 + (6 × 9) =** | **(54 ÷ 6) × (3 + 17) =**

How many times greater or smaller is the second number compared to the first?

| 0.09 | 700,000 | 300 | 0.006 |
| 900 | 7,000 | 0.03 | 0.6 |

_____ | _____ | _____ | _____

What is the volume?

 = 1 cubic unit

_____ cubic units | _____ cubic units | _____ cubic units | _____ cubic units

Name _____ Date _____

Evaluate each expression.

| (72 ÷ 9) × (15 − 8) = | 300 × (18 ÷ 6) = | 9 × (6 + 2) = |

How many times greater or smaller is the second number compared to the first?

| 30 | 600,000 | 4,000 |
| 0.3 | 6,000,000 | 0.4 |

_____   _____   _____

What is the volume?

 = 1 cubic unit

_____ cubic units   _____ cubic units   _____ cubic units

Convert each mixed number to an improper fraction.

$3\frac{1}{4}$ = $2\frac{5}{6}$ = $8\frac{1}{2}$ =

Name _____ Date _____

Evaluate each expression.

459 + (4 × 5) = | 500 × (50 ÷ 5) = | (42 ÷ 6) × (25 × 2) = | (90 ÷ 3) × (5 × 8) =

How many times greater or smaller is the second number compared to the first?

| 0.006 | 70 | 800,000 | 40 |
| 600 | 0.07 | 80 | 4,000,000 |

_____ | _____ | _____ | _____

What is the volume?

 = 1 cubic unit

   | | 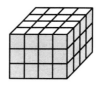 |

_____ cubic units | _____ cubic units | _____ cubic units | _____ cubic units

---

Convert each mixed number to an improper fraction.

$7\frac{5}{8} =$ | $8\frac{6}{7} =$ | $10\frac{5}{6} =$ | $6\frac{5}{9} =$

Name _____ **Date** _____

How many times greater or smaller is the second number compared to the first?

| **50** | **90** | **200** |
| **0.5** | **90,000** | **2,000,000** |

_____ | _____ | _____

What is the volume?

 = 1 cubic unit

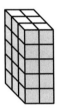

_____ cubic units | _____ cubic units | _____ cubic units

Convert each mixed number to an improper fraction.

$4 \frac{3}{4} =$ $2 \frac{8}{9} =$ $5 \frac{1}{5} =$

Convert each improper fraction to a mixed number.

$\frac{15}{4} =$ $\frac{16}{5} =$ $\frac{17}{6} =$

Name _____ Date _____

How many times greater or smaller is the second number compared to the first?

3,000	0.009	70	0.5
0.03	90	700,000	50,000

_____ | _____ | _____ | _____

What is the volume?

 = 1 cubic unit

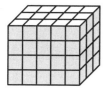   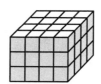

_____ cubic units | _____ cubic units | _____ cubic units | _____ cubic units

Convert each mixed number to an improper fraction.

$7\frac{5}{6} =$ $8\frac{5}{9} =$ $6\frac{2}{9} =$ $9\frac{3}{8} =$

Convert each improper fraction to a mixed number.

$\frac{50}{6} =$ $\frac{45}{7} =$ $\frac{83}{9} =$ $\frac{60}{7} =$

Name _____ **Date** _____

What is the volume?

 = 1 cubic unit

_____ cubic units   _____ cubic units   _____ cubic units

Convert each mixed number to an improper fraction.

$5\frac{2}{5} =$ $10\frac{2}{3} =$ $8\frac{1}{2} =$

Convert each improper fraction to a mixed number.

$\frac{9}{2} =$ $\frac{17}{4} =$ $\frac{32}{7} =$

Round each number to the nearest …

… tenth.   … hundredth.   … tenth.

3.825   **5.237**   **586.451**

Name _____ Date _____

What is the volume?

 = 1 cubic unit

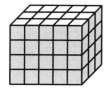

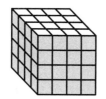

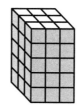

_____ cubic units   _____ cubic units   _____ cubic units   _____ cubic units

Convert each mixed number to an improper fraction.

$9\frac{5}{6} =$ $8\frac{4}{5} =$ $7\frac{6}{8} =$ $9\frac{5}{7} =$

Convert each improper fraction to a mixed number.

$\frac{55}{7} =$ $\frac{61}{8} =$ $\frac{43}{5} =$ $\frac{80}{9} =$

Round each number to the nearest …

… hundredth.   … thousandth.   … tenth.   … hundredth.

45.2683   **33.6081**   **59.2748**   **62.9551**

Name _____ **Date** _____

Convert each mixed number to an improper fraction.

$7\dfrac{3}{4} =$ $6\dfrac{1}{8} =$ $9\dfrac{5}{9} =$

Convert each improper fraction to a mixed number.

$\dfrac{26}{3} =$ $\dfrac{49}{5} =$ $\dfrac{75}{8} =$

Round each number to the nearest …

… tenth.

681.725

… whole number.

18.497

… hundredth.

253.786

Add the fractions.

$\dfrac{2}{3} + \dfrac{1}{9} =$ $\dfrac{2}{5} + \dfrac{3}{10} =$ $\dfrac{4}{7} + \dfrac{3}{21} =$

Name _____ **Date** _____

Convert each mixed number to an improper fraction.

$9\dfrac{5}{7} =$ | $8\dfrac{7}{8} =$ | $7\dfrac{4}{7} =$ | $6\dfrac{4}{9} =$

Convert each improper fraction to a mixed number.

$\dfrac{86}{9} =$ | $\dfrac{37}{4} =$ | $\dfrac{23}{3} =$ | $\dfrac{39}{4} =$

Round each number to the nearest …

… whole number.	… thousandth.	… hundredth.	… tenth.
215.7176	38.2567	52.7834	16.293

Add the fractions.

$\dfrac{4}{7} + \dfrac{3}{10} =$ | $\dfrac{3}{4} + \dfrac{1}{9} =$ | $\dfrac{1}{5} + \dfrac{5}{8} =$ | $\dfrac{2}{7} + \dfrac{1}{3} =$

Name _____ Date _____

Convert each improper fraction to a mixed number.

$$\frac{35}{4} =$$

$$\frac{23}{7} =$$

$$\frac{44}{5} =$$

Round each number to the nearest …

… tenth.

52.718

… whole number.

3.641

… hundredth.

218.4526

Add the fractions.

$$\frac{3}{5} + \frac{3}{10} =$$

$$\frac{5}{12} + \frac{1}{6} =$$

$$\frac{2}{3} + \frac{1}{5} =$$

Convert numbers with exponents to whole numbers and whole numbers to numbers with exponents.

$$10^4 =$$

$$100 =$$

$$10^3 =$$

Name _____ Date _____

Convert each improper fraction to a mixed number.

$\dfrac{62}{7} =$ $\dfrac{59}{6} =$ $\dfrac{49}{8} =$ $\dfrac{52}{9} =$

Round each number to the nearest …

… tenth.	… whole number.	… hundredth.	… thousandth.
785.512	**25.394**	**6.2891**	**2.31574**

Add the fractions.

$\dfrac{3}{8} + \dfrac{4}{7} =$ $\dfrac{3}{4} + \dfrac{1}{10} =$ $\dfrac{1}{7} + \dfrac{5}{14} =$ $\dfrac{4}{5} + \dfrac{1}{9} =$

Convert numbers with exponents to whole numbers
and whole numbers to numbers with exponents.

$10^5 =$ $1{,}000 =$ $10^2 =$ $1{,}000{,}000 =$

Name _____ **Date** _____

Round each number to the nearest …

… thousandth.	… tenth.	… whole number.
6.2814	**2.9394**	**541.683**

Add the fractions.

$\dfrac{1}{2} + \dfrac{1}{8} =$ $\qquad$ $\dfrac{2}{5} + \dfrac{3}{20} =$ $\qquad$ $\dfrac{5}{9} + \dfrac{3}{18} =$

Convert numbers with exponents to whole numbers
and whole numbers to numbers with exponents.

$10^3 =$ $\qquad$ $100 =$ $\qquad$ $10^4 =$

Use exponents to complete each equation.

$10^3 \times 10^2 =$ $\qquad$ $10^5 \times 10^3 =$ $\qquad$ $10^4 \times 10^1 =$

Name _____ Date _____

Round each number to the nearest …

… thousandth.	… tenth.	… whole number.	… hundredth.
15.2984	32.5625	28.439	52.6481

Add the fractions.

$\frac{3}{7} + \frac{5}{9} =$ $\frac{4}{9} + \frac{3}{10} =$ $\frac{3}{8} + \frac{1}{16} =$ $\frac{4}{5} + \frac{1}{8} =$

Convert numbers with exponents to whole numbers
and whole numbers to numbers with exponents.

$10^5 =$ $10,000 =$ $10^6 =$ $100 =$

Use exponents to complete each equation.

$10^7 \times \quad = 10^{12}$ $\quad \times 10^2 = 10^8$ $10^3 \times 10^5 =$ $10^5 \times \quad = 10^{14}$

Name _____ **Date** _____

Add the fractions.

$\frac{2}{3} + \frac{1}{9} =$ $\frac{1}{4} + \frac{3}{7} =$ $\frac{3}{10} + \frac{1}{2} =$

Convert numbers with exponents to whole numbers
and whole numbers to numbers with exponents.

$10^6 =$ $1,000 =$ $10^2 =$

Use exponents to complete each equation.

$10^6 \times 10^3 =$ $10^2 \times 10^2 =$ $10^1 \times 10^1 =$

Using decimals, write an addition equation that describes what part of each model is shaded.

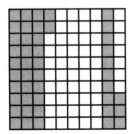   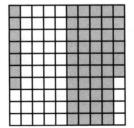   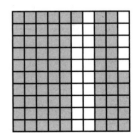

_____   _____   _____

Name _____ Date _____

Add the fractions.

$\frac{5}{21} + \frac{4}{7} =$　　$\frac{3}{4} + \frac{1}{9} =$　　$\frac{14}{25} + \frac{2}{5} =$　　$\frac{1}{5} + \frac{3}{4} =$

Convert numbers with exponents to whole numbers
and whole numbers to numbers with exponents.

$10^5 =$　　$100 =$　　$10^3 =$　　$10,000 =$

Use exponents to complete each equation.

$10^5 \times \underline{\hspace{1cm}} = 10^{11}$　　$\underline{\hspace{1cm}} \times 10^3 = 10^8$　　$10^6 \times 10^7 = \underline{\hspace{1cm}}$　　$\underline{\hspace{1cm}} \times 10^2 = 10^9$

Using decimals, write an addition equation that describes what part of each model is shaded.

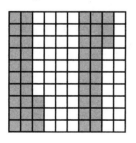　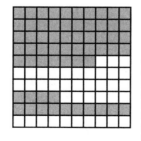　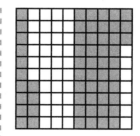　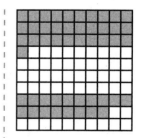

_____　_____　_____　_____

Name _____ Date _____

Convert numbers with exponents to whole numbers
and whole numbers to numbers with exponents.

$10^2 =$

$10,000 =$

$10^5 =$

Use exponents to complete each equation.

$10^4 \times 10^5 =$

$10^8 \times 10^7 =$

$10^3 \times 10^3 =$

Using decimals, write an addition equation that describes what part of each model is shaded.

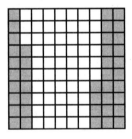

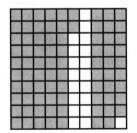

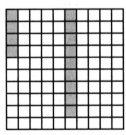

_____

_____

_____

What is the outcome?

8 | + 3 |⇨ | ×2 |⇨ | − 6 |⇨

_____

12 | ×2 |⇨ | + 25 |⇨ | − 17 |⇨

What are the missing functions?

8 [   ]⇨ 13 [   ]⇨ 26

9 [   ]⇨ 14 [   ]⇨ 28

10 [   ]⇨ 15 [   ]⇨ 30

Name _____ **Date** _____

Convert numbers with exponents to whole numbers
and whole numbers to numbers with exponents.

$10^7 =$ | $1,000,000 =$ | $10^8 =$ | $10,000 =$

Use exponents to complete each equation.

$10^5 \times 10^9 =$ | $10^3 \times = 10^5$ | $10^3 \times 10^4 =$ | $ \times 10^3 = 10^8$

Using decimals, write an addition equation that describes what part of each model is shaded.

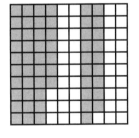 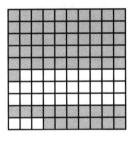 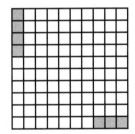 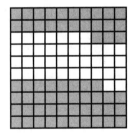

_____ | _____ | _____ | _____

What is the outcome? | What are the missing functions?

9 [× 4] ▷ [÷ 6] ▷ [+ 29] ▷

_____

63 [÷ 9] ▷ [× 8] ▷ [+ 17] ▷

8 [ ] ▷ 24 [ ] ▷ 31 [ ] ▷ 27

10 [ ] ▷ 30 [ ] ▷ 37 [ ] ▷ 33

15 [ ] ▷ 45 [ ] ▷ 52 [ ] ▷ 48

Name _____ **Date** _____

Use exponents to complete each equation.

$10^3 \times 10^2 =$ $10^4 \times 10^7 =$ $10^8 \times 10^2 =$

Using decimals, write an addition equation that describes what part of each model is shaded.

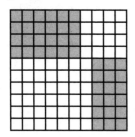   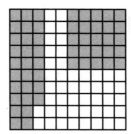   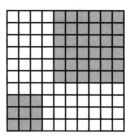

_____   _____   _____

What is the outcome?

8 | × 7 ▷ | + 7 ▷ | ÷ 9 ▷

_____

8 | + 10 ▷ | ÷ 6 ▷ | × 9 ▷

What are the missing functions?

24 [ ] ▷ 6 [ ] ▷ 36

36 [ ] ▷ 9 [ ] ▷ 54

12 [ ] ▷ 3 [ ] ▷ 18

Subtract the fractions.

$\dfrac{3}{10} - \dfrac{1}{5} =$ $\dfrac{2}{3} - \dfrac{1}{9} =$ $\dfrac{3}{4} - \dfrac{1}{2} =$

Name _____ **Date** _____

Use exponents to complete each equation.

$10^5 \times 10^2 =$ $10^8 \times$ ___ $= 10^{11}$ ___ $\times 10^6 = 10^{10}$ $10^3 \times 10^9 =$

Using decimals, write an addition equation that describes what part of each model is shaded.

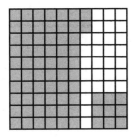 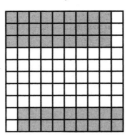 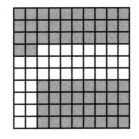 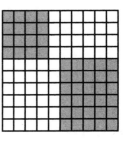

_____   _____   _____   _____

What is the outcome?

9 [× 11]▷   [+ 21]▷   [÷ 4]▷

_____

63 [+ 18]▷   [÷ 9]▷   [× 7]▷

What are the missing functions?

4 [ ] ▷ 36   [ ] ▷ 12   [ ] ▷ 31

10 [ ] ▷ 90   [ ] ▷ 30   [ ] ▷ 49

2 [ ] ▷ 18   [ ] ▷ 6   [ ] ▷ 25

Subtract the fractions.

$\dfrac{7}{9} - \dfrac{1}{2} =$ $\dfrac{3}{4} - \dfrac{1}{8} =$ $\dfrac{4}{5} - \dfrac{3}{8} =$ $\dfrac{19}{20} - \dfrac{2}{5} =$

Name _____ Date _____

Using decimals, write an addition equation that describes what part of each model is shaded.

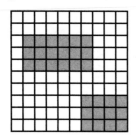 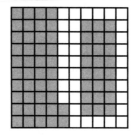 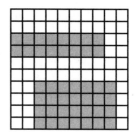

_____ _____ _____

What is the outcome?

17 | + 4 ⇨ | ÷ 3 ⇨ | × 6 ⇨

_____

12 | + 24 ⇨ | × 2 ⇨ | ÷ 9 ⇨

What are the missing functions?

21 [   ] ⇨ 27 [   ] ⇨ 9

9 [   ] ⇨ 15 [   ] ⇨ 5

24 [   ] ⇨ 30 [   ] ⇨ 10

Subtract the fractions.

$\dfrac{5}{8} - \dfrac{1}{4} =$ $\dfrac{5}{6} - \dfrac{9}{12} =$ $\dfrac{2}{3} - \dfrac{1}{10} =$

What is the quotient?

$3 \div \dfrac{1}{4} =$ $5 \div \dfrac{1}{2} =$ $7 \div \dfrac{1}{4} =$

Name _____ Date _____

Using decimals, write an addition equation that describes what part of each model is shaded.

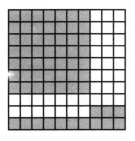 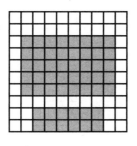 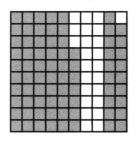 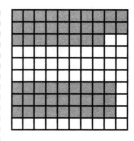

_____ | _____ | _____ | _____

What is the outcome?

5 | × 9 ⇨ | × 7 ⇨ | ÷ 3 ⇨

_____

26 | + 59 ⇨ | ÷ 5 ⇨ | × 7 ⇨

What are the missing functions?

72 [ ] ⇨ 8 [ ] ⇨ 27 [ ] ⇨ 54

54 [ ] ⇨ 6 [ ] ⇨ 25 [ ] ⇨ 52

81 [ ] ⇨ 9 [ ] ⇨ 28 [ ] ⇨ 55

Subtract the fractions.

$\dfrac{1}{3} - \dfrac{2}{7} =$ | $\dfrac{6}{9} - \dfrac{7}{18} =$ | $\dfrac{19}{24} - \dfrac{3}{12} =$ | $\dfrac{7}{9} - \dfrac{5}{10} =$

What is the quotient?

$8 \div \dfrac{1}{7} =$ | $9 \div \dfrac{1}{6} =$ | $7 \div \dfrac{1}{6} =$ | $9 \div \dfrac{1}{4} =$

Name _____ Date _____

What is the outcome?

26 | + 19 ▷ | × 2 ▷ | ÷ 3 ▷

_____

91 | − 16 ▷ | ÷ 3 ▷ | × 4 ▷

What are the missing functions?

3 [ ] ▷ 19 [ ] ▷ 57

12 [ ] ▷ 28 [ ] ▷ 84

5 [ ] ▷ 21 [ ] ▷ 63

Subtract the fractions.

$\frac{7}{10} - \frac{2}{5} =$

$\frac{3}{4} - \frac{1}{3} =$

$\frac{11}{15} - \frac{3}{5} =$

What is the quotient?

$8 \div \frac{1}{5} =$

$9 \div \frac{1}{3} =$

$5 \div \frac{1}{4} =$

What is the sum?

4.28 + 23.7 =

86 + 4.92 =

2.76 + 38.54 =

Name _____ Date _____

What is the outcome?

29 | x 3 ▷ | – 19 ▷ | ÷ 2 ▷

_____

29 | – 19 ▷ | x 3 ▷ | ÷ 2 ▷

What are the missing functions?

28 | ☐ ▷ 7 | ☐ ▷ 30 | ☐ ▷ 120

44 | ☐ ▷ 11 | ☐ ▷ 34 | ☐ ▷ 136

12 | ☐ ▷ 3 | ☐ ▷ 26 | ☐ ▷ 104

Subtract the fractions.

$\dfrac{2}{3} - \dfrac{2}{7} =$

$\dfrac{10}{24} - \dfrac{1}{8} =$

$\dfrac{7}{9} - \dfrac{2}{7} =$

$\dfrac{13}{18} - \dfrac{4}{9} =$

What is the quotient?

$12 \div \dfrac{1}{8} =$

$15 \div \dfrac{1}{2} =$

$6 \div \dfrac{1}{10} =$

$9 \div \dfrac{1}{6} =$

What is the sum?

$23.84 + 4.6 =$ $295 + 8.37 =$ $53 + 29.64 =$ $8.21 + 56.45 =$

Name _____ **Date** _____

Subtract the fractions.

$$\frac{2}{3} - \frac{1}{5} =$$ $$\frac{5}{8} - \frac{1}{4} =$$ $$\frac{7}{8} - \frac{1}{2} =$$

What is the quotient?

$$7 \div \frac{1}{7} =$$ $$2 \div \frac{1}{10} =$$ $$8 \div \frac{1}{3} =$$

What is the sum?

$$2.63 + 23.7 =$$ $$108.6 + 5.72 =$$ $$59.73 + 6.9 =$$

Determine the volume of each rectangular prism.

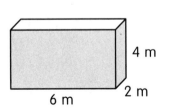
4 m
2 m
6 m

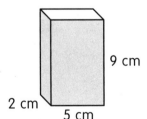
9 cm
2 cm
5 cm

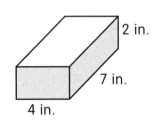
2 in.
7 in.
4 in.

Week-by-Week Math Review for the Digital Classroom: Grade 5 • © 2015 by Steve Wyborney, Scholastic Teaching Resources

Name _____ **Date** _____

Subtract the fractions.

$$\frac{7}{9} - \frac{1}{18} =$$ $$\frac{4}{9} - \frac{2}{7} =$$ $$\frac{11}{12} - \frac{17}{24} =$$ $$\frac{7}{8} - \frac{5}{7} =$$

What is the quotient?

$$8 \div \frac{1}{6} =$$ $$9 \div \frac{1}{8} =$$ $$7 \div \frac{1}{6} =$$ $$4 \div \frac{1}{8} =$$

What is the sum?

$$32.498 + 6.27 =$$ $$81.54 + 238.7 =$$ $$629.18 + 2.794 =$$ $$0.29 + 58.84 =$$

Determine the volume of each rectangular prism.

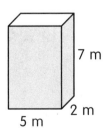 7 m, 2 m, 5 m

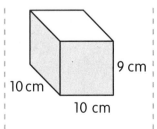 9 cm, 10 cm, 10 cm

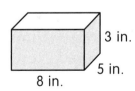 3 in., 5 in., 8 in.

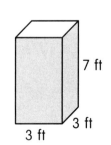 7 ft, 3 ft, 3 ft

_____   _____   _____   _____

Name _____ Date _____

What is the quotient?

$5 \div \frac{1}{2} =$ $4 \div \frac{1}{3} =$ $7 \div \frac{1}{5} =$

What is the sum?

52.67 + 28.45 =   9.918 + 624.3 =   159 + 72.5 =

Determine the volume of each rectangular prism.

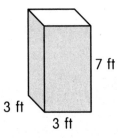
7 ft
3 ft
3 ft

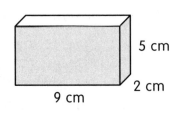
5 cm
2 cm
9 cm

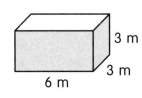
3 m
3 m
6 m

_____   _____   _____

Determine the value of the variable in each equation.

4 × (3 + 6) = m   d × (5 + 2) = 56   32 ÷ (9 − b) = 4

42

Name _____ Date _____

What is the quotient?

$8 \div \frac{1}{7} =$ $12 \div \frac{1}{5} =$ $8 \div \frac{1}{9} =$ $6 \div \frac{1}{7} =$

What is the sum?

2.714 + 328.5 =   **614 + 2.68 =**   **53.54 + 8.7 =**   **54.29 + 1.085 =**

Determine the volume of each rectangular prism.

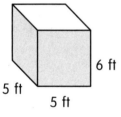

5 ft   6 ft   5 ft

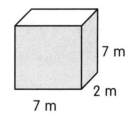

4 cm   3 cm   6 cm

7 m   2 m   7 m

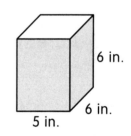

6 in.   6 in.   5 in.

_____   _____   _____   _____

Determine the value of the variable in each equation.

(5 + 2) × (4 + 5) = s   **m − (6 × 4) = 7**   **(4 + c) ÷ 3 = 5**   **b × (6 + 3) = 36**

Weekly Week Math Review for the Digital Classroom, Grade 5 © 2015 by Steve Wyborney, Scholastic Teaching Resources

Name _____ Date _____

What is the sum?

| 52.83 + 7.352 = | 884 + 8.84 = | 7.183 + 168.3 = |

Determine the volume of each rectangular prism.

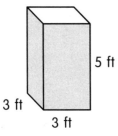

5 ft

3 ft

3 ft

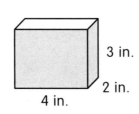

3 in.

2 in.

4 in.

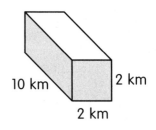

10 km

2 km

2 km

_____   _____   _____

Determine the value of the variable in each equation.

| s + (10 − 3) = 15 | (20 + 20) ÷ n = 8 | (9 × 9) + (3 × 3) = m |

Using decimals, write the subtraction equation that each model represents.

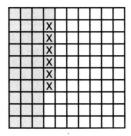

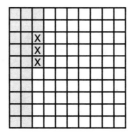

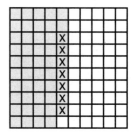

_____   _____   _____

Name _____ Date _____

What is the sum?

| 7.593 + 26.83 = | 2.647 + 541.7 = | 2.018 + 674 = | 526 + 29.87 = |

Determine the volume of each rectangular prism.

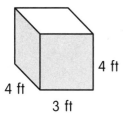 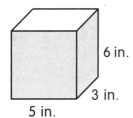 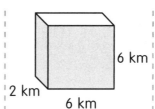 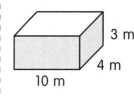

_____   _____   _____   _____

Determine the value of the variable in each equation.

| (5 + 2) × (4 + s) = 49 | m − (7 × 5) = 4 | (3 + c) ÷ 5 = 8 | 4 × (3 + b) = 28 |

Using decimals, write the subtraction equation that each model represents.

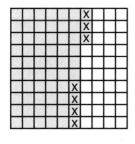 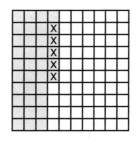

_____   _____   _____   _____

Name _____ Date _____

Determine the volume of each rectangular prism.

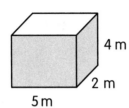

4 m

2 m

5 m

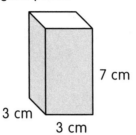

7 cm

3 cm

3 cm

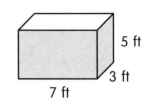

5 ft

3 ft

7 ft

_____   _____   _____

Determine the value of the variable in each equation.

$8 \times (10 - 4) = m$ $(11 - 4) \times s = 56$ $(8 \div 2) \times (3 \times 4) = c$

Using decimals, write the subtraction equation that each model represents.

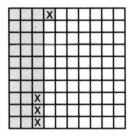

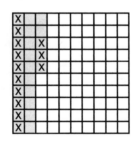

_____   _____   _____

Determine the quotient.

$\dfrac{1}{4} \div 3 =$ $\dfrac{1}{5} \div 4 =$ $\dfrac{1}{3} \div 6 =$

Name _____ **Date** _____

Determine the volume of each rectangular prism.

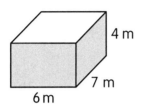 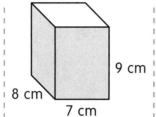 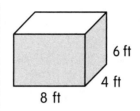 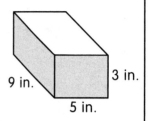

_____   _____   _____   _____

Determine the value of the variable in each equation.

$m \times (48 \div 8) = 42$ $(s - 4) \div 3 = 5$ $(6 + 2) \times (5 + c) = 56$ $y - (9 + 9) = 3$

Using decimals, write the subtraction equation that each model represents.

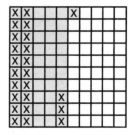 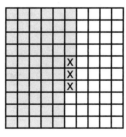

_____   _____   _____   _____

Determine the quotient.

$\dfrac{1}{9} \div 4 =$ $\dfrac{1}{6} \div 7 =$ $\dfrac{1}{8} \div 3 =$ $\dfrac{1}{5} \div 9 =$

Name _____ Date _____

Determine the value of the variable in each equation.

| c × (3 + 4) = 35 | (20 – 12) × s = 24 | (7 × 8) – (5 × 5) = m |

Using decimals, write the subtraction equation that each model represents.

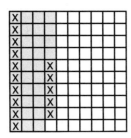 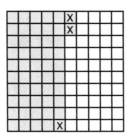 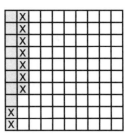

_____   _____   _____

Determine the quotient.

$$\frac{1}{7} \div 2 =$$ $$\frac{1}{2} \div 5 =$$ $$\frac{1}{6} \div 4 =$$

Write an ordered pair to describe the location of each point.

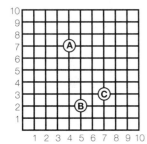 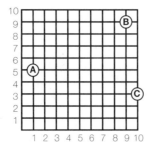 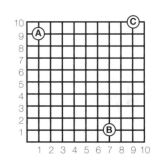

_____   _____   _____

Name _____ **Date** _____

Determine the value of the variable in each equation.

$8 \times (h - 2) = 48$ | $(52 - 31) \times m = 84$ | $(5 + 4) \times (3 + c) = 54$ | $n \times (2 + 7) = 90$

Using decimals, write the subtraction equation that each model represents.

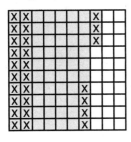 | 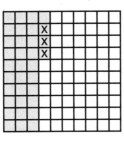 | 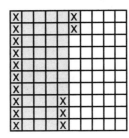 |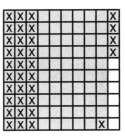

_____ | _____ | _____ | _____

Determine the quotient.

$\dfrac{1}{9} \div 9 =$ | $\dfrac{1}{10} \div 4 =$ | $\dfrac{1}{8} \div 7 =$ | $\dfrac{1}{10} \div 6 =$

Write an ordered pair to describe the location of each point.

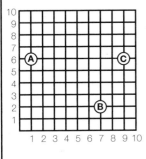 | 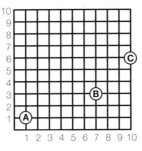 | 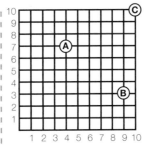 |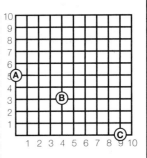

_____ | _____ | _____ | _____

Name _____ Date _____

Using decimals, write the subtraction equation that each model represents.

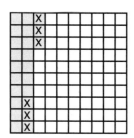

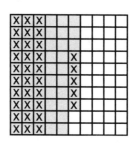

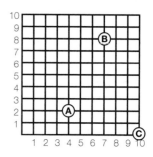

_____   _____   _____

Determine the quotient.

$$\frac{1}{4} \div 5 =$$ $$\frac{1}{7} \div 3 =$$ $$\frac{1}{3} \div 6 =$$

Write an ordered pair to describe the location of each point.

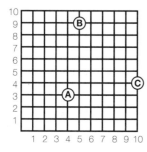

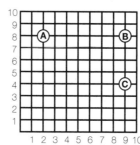

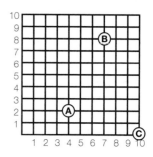

_____   _____   _____

What is the difference?

38.7 – 21.8 =   **25.43 – 7.6 =**   **15.7 – 3.24 =**

Name _____ Date _____

Using decimals, write the subtraction equation that each model represents.

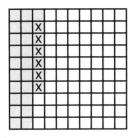 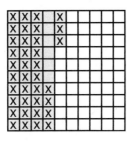 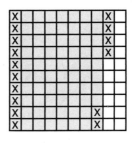 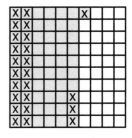

_____ _____ _____ _____

Determine the quotient.

$$\frac{1}{9} \div 6 =$$ $$\frac{1}{8} \div 7 =$$ $$\frac{1}{7} \div 7 =$$ $$\frac{1}{6} \div 8 =$$

Write an ordered pair to describe the location of each point.

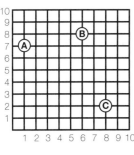 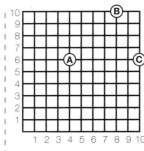 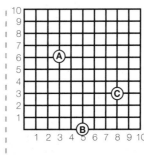 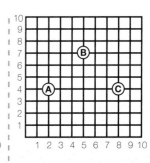

_____ _____ _____ _____

What is the difference?

45 – 7.2 = **59.4 – 3.27 =** **89.7 – 3.5 =** **6.27 – 0.36 =**

Name _____ Date _____

Determine the quotient.

$\frac{1}{2} \div 2 =$

$\frac{1}{4} \div 6 =$

$\frac{1}{8} \div 3 =$

Write an ordered pair to describe the location of each point.

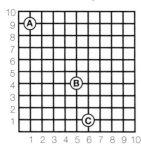

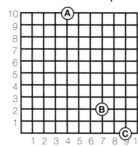

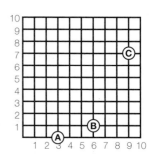

_____   _____   _____

What is the difference?

$84 - 3.5 =$

$67.4 - 2.61 =$

$85.61 - 2.5 =$

Determine the volume.

 = 1 cubic unit

_____ cubic units   _____ cubic units   _____ cubic units

Week-by-Week Math Review for the Digital Classroom: Grade 3 © 2015 by Steve Wyborney, Scholastic Teaching Resources

Name _____ **Date** _____

Determine the quotient.

$\frac{1}{10} \div 4 =$

$\frac{1}{8} \div 8 =$

$\frac{1}{7} \div 4 =$

$\frac{1}{3} \div 9 =$

Write an ordered pair to describe the location of each point.

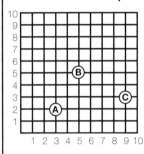

_____

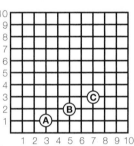

_____

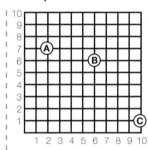

_____

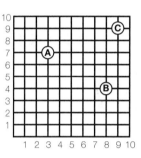

_____

What is the difference?

$26 - 0.26 =$

$8.8 - 0.88 =$

$97.52 - 52.3 =$

$67 - 0.21 =$

Determine the volume.

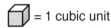 = 1 cubic unit

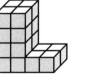

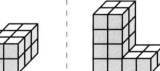

_____ cubic units

_____ cubic units

_____ cubic units

_____ cubic units

Name _____ Date _____

Write an ordered pair to describe the location of each point.

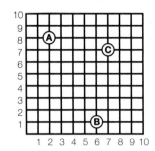

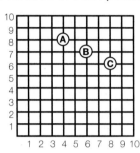

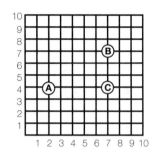

_____   _____   _____

What is the difference?

18.7 – 5.8 =   **9.26 – 1.83 =**   **54 – 6.3 =**

Determine the volume.

 = 1 cubic unit

_____ cubic units   _____ cubic units   _____ cubic units

Determine the product.

```
    32              51              46
  × 43            × 28            × 32
  ____            ____            ____
```

Name _____ **Date** _____

Write an ordered pair to describe the location of each point.

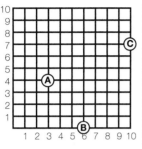 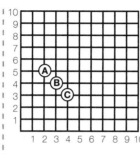 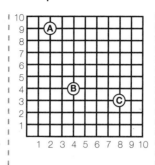 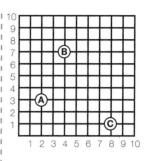

_____ _____ _____ _____

What is the difference?

46 – 9.53 =	**18.91 – 2.6 =**	**39.23 – 21.86 =**	**458.7 – 325 =**

Determine the volume.

 = 1 cubic unit

  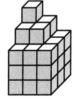

_____ cubic units   _____ cubic units   _____ cubic units   _____ cubic units

Determine the product.

86	78	274	543
× 54	× 53	× 16	× 29

Name _____ Date _____

What is the difference?

| 78.35 – 21.18 = | 62 – 5.7 = | 48.6 – 29 = |

Determine the volume.

 = 1 cubic unit

_____ cubic units   _____ cubic units   _____ cubic units

Determine the product.

| 36 $\times$ 24 | 59 $\times$ 16 | 21 $\times$ 95 |

Determine an equal measurement.

| 1 m = 100 cm | 1 foot = 12 in. | 1 yard = 3 ft |

7 meters   5 feet   15 yards

= _____ cm   = _____ in.   = _____ ft

Name _____ **Date** _____

What is the difference?

| 86 – 13.25 = | 27.94 – 2.8 = | 154.2 – 26.7 = | 43.8 – 2.79 = |

Determine the volume.

 = 1 cubic unit

   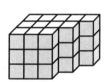

_____ cubic units | _____ cubic units | _____ cubic units | _____ cubic units

---

Determine the product.

| 58 | 65 | 64 | 289 |
| × 97 | × 83 | × 67 | × 75 |

Determine an equal measurement.

| **9 meters** | **8 feet** | **23 yards** | **14 yards** |
| = _____ cm | = _____ in. | = _____ ft | = _____ in. |

Name _____ **Date** _____

Determine the volume.

 = 1 cubic unit

_____ cubic units   _____ cubic units   _____ cubic units

Determine the product.

53 × 29	61 × 55	62 × 48

Determine an equal measurement.

1 gallon = 4 qts	1 mile = 1,760 yds	1 week = 7 days
17 gallons	8 miles	52 weeks
= _____ qts	= _____ yds	= _____ days

Compare the decimals. Use <, >, or =.

3.56 ◯ 35.6   6.21 ◯ 62.1   49.28 ◯ 49.28

Name _____ **Date** _____

Determine the volume.

 = 1 cubic unit

_____ cubic units   _____ cubic units   _____ cubic units   _____ cubic units

---

Determine the product.

86 × 54	98 × 74	296 × 52	816 × 93

Determine an equal measurement.

29 gallons   **9 miles**   **324 weeks**   **8 miles**

= _____ qts   = _____ yds   = _____ days   = _____ ft

Compare the decimals. Use <, >, or =.

2.51 ◯ 2.15   384.96 ◯ 383.97   23.17 ◯ 23.4   83.9 ◯ 83.11

Name _____ Date _____

Determine the product.

$$\begin{array}{r} 45 \\ \times\ 16 \\ \hline \end{array}$$

$$\begin{array}{r} 83 \\ \times\ 52 \\ \hline \end{array}$$

$$\begin{array}{r} 37 \\ \times\ 64 \\ \hline \end{array}$$

Determine an equal measurement.

| 1 km = 1,000 m | 1 foot = 12 in. | 1 yard = 3 ft |

19 km

23 feet

73 yards

= _____ m

= _____ in.

= _____ ft

Compare the decimals. Use <, >, or =.

63.29 ◯ 63.92

7.45 ◯ 7.6

258.16 ◯ 258.31

Determine the product.

$\dfrac{2}{3} \times \dfrac{2}{5} =$

$\dfrac{1}{3} \times \dfrac{7}{8} =$

$\dfrac{2}{5} \times \dfrac{3}{5} =$

Name _____ **Date** _____

Determine the product.

$$\begin{array}{r} 36 \\ \times\ 97 \\ \hline \end{array} \qquad \begin{array}{r} 74 \\ \times\ 18 \\ \hline \end{array} \qquad \begin{array}{r} 284 \\ \times\ 68 \\ \hline \end{array} \qquad \begin{array}{r} 597 \\ \times\ 83 \\ \hline \end{array}$$

Determine an equal measurement.

73 km   **567 feet**   **218 yards**   **56 yards**

= _____ m   = _____ in.   = _____ ft   = _____ in.

Compare the decimals. Use <, >, or =.

98 ◯ 97.46   3.02 ◯ 3.1   181 ◯ 181.3   67.4 ◯ 67.13

Determine the product.

$$\frac{7}{8} \times \frac{3}{9} = \qquad \frac{5}{7} \times \frac{7}{9} = \qquad \frac{3}{4} \times \frac{3}{4} = \qquad \frac{2}{9} \times \frac{6}{7} =$$

Name _____ **Date** _____

Determine an equal measurement.

1 gallon = 4 qts	1 mile = 1,760 yds	1 week = 7 days

255 gallons

= _____ qts

8 miles

= _____ yds

45 weeks

= _____ days

Compare the decimals. Use <, >, or =.

28.6 $\bigcirc$ 28

4.23 $\bigcirc$ 4.237

81.27 $\bigcirc$ 81.72

Determine the product.

$\frac{3}{7} \times \frac{4}{5} =$

$\frac{2}{3} \times \frac{5}{6} =$

$\frac{7}{10} \times \frac{2}{3} =$

Determine the product.

$$\begin{array}{r} 0.4 \\ \times\ 0.6 \\ \hline \end{array}$$

$$\begin{array}{r} 8 \\ \times\ 0.7 \\ \hline \end{array}$$

$$\begin{array}{r} 7 \\ \times\ 0.3 \\ \hline \end{array}$$

Week-by-Week Math Review for the Digital Classroom: Grade 5 © 2015 by Steve Wyborney; Scholastic Teaching Resources

Name _____ Date _____

Determine an equal measurement.

96 gallons	7 miles	215 weeks	16 miles
= _____ qts	= _____ yds	= _____ days	= _____ ft

Compare the decimals. Use <, >, or =.

46.38 ◯ 46.83   2.715 ◯ 2.94   3.67 ◯ 3.274   8.104 ◯ 8.26

Determine the product.

$$\frac{8}{9} \times \frac{6}{7} =$$ $$\frac{4}{5} \times \frac{7}{9} =$$ $$\frac{7}{8} \times \frac{2}{7} =$$ $$\frac{5}{6} \times \frac{6}{7} =$$

Determine the product.

0.04	0.2	0.009	0.7
× 0.7	× 0.9	× 5	× 0.7

Name _____ **Date** _____

Compare the decimals. Use <, >, or =.

48.06 $\bigcirc$ 48.07   29.35 $\bigcirc$ 29.4   451.3 $\bigcirc$ 450.88

Determine the product.

$\dfrac{4}{5} \times \dfrac{4}{7} =$ $\dfrac{3}{7} \times \dfrac{2}{5} =$ $\dfrac{5}{8} \times \dfrac{2}{3} =$

Determine the product.

$$\begin{array}{r} 8 \\ \times\ 0.4 \\ \hline \end{array}$$

$$\begin{array}{r} 0.4 \\ \times\ 0.7 \\ \hline \end{array}$$

$$\begin{array}{r} 0.004 \\ \times\qquad 3 \\ \hline \end{array}$$

Determine the quotient.

$4\overline{)3.2}$ $0.5\overline{)0.45}$ $0.6\overline{)1.8}$

Name _____ Date _____

Compare the decimals. Use <, >, or =.

28.394 ◯ 38.349 | 36 ◯ 36.001 | 851.34 ◯ 851.298 | 63.91 ◯ 63.901

Determine the product.

$\dfrac{8}{9} \times \dfrac{1}{7} =$ | $\dfrac{6}{7} \times \dfrac{4}{5} =$ | $\dfrac{7}{8} \times \dfrac{8}{9} =$ | $\dfrac{2}{5} \times \dfrac{3}{4} =$

Determine the product.

$$\begin{array}{r} 0.7 \\ \times\ 0.3 \\ \hline \end{array}$$ | $$\begin{array}{r} 0.2 \\ \times\ 0.03 \\ \hline \end{array}$$ | $$\begin{array}{r} 0.09 \\ \times\quad 7 \\ \hline \end{array}$$ | $$\begin{array}{r} 5 \\ \times\ 0.9 \\ \hline \end{array}$$

Determine the quotient.

$9 \overline{)\,5.4}$ | $0.8 \overline{)\,7.2}$ | $0.03 \overline{)\,2.4}$ | $0.5 \overline{)\,0.35}$

Name _____ Date _____

Determine the product.

$$\frac{3}{5} \times \frac{1}{8} =$$

$$\frac{3}{4} \times \frac{3}{4} =$$

$$\frac{7}{8} \times \frac{1}{2} =$$

Determine the product.

$$\begin{array}{r} 0.8 \\ \times\, 0.4 \\ \hline \end{array}$$

$$\begin{array}{r} 9 \\ \times\, 0.5 \\ \hline \end{array}$$

$$\begin{array}{r} 0.003 \\ \times\quad 9 \\ \hline \end{array}$$

Determine the quotient.

$$8 \overline{)4.8}$$

$$0.7 \overline{)0.42}$$

$$0.9 \overline{)2.7}$$

Determine the product.

$$2\frac{3}{4} \times \frac{1}{2} =$$

$$\frac{2}{3} \times 3\frac{1}{2} =$$

$$4\frac{1}{3} \times \frac{2}{7} =$$

Name _____ Date _____

Determine the product.

$\dfrac{6}{7} \times \dfrac{6}{7} =$ $\dfrac{3}{8} \times \dfrac{5}{6} =$ $\dfrac{5}{6} \times \dfrac{7}{9} =$ $\dfrac{7}{8} \times \dfrac{4}{5} =$

Determine the product.

$$\begin{array}{r} 9 \\ \times\, 0.07 \\ \hline \end{array}$$ $$\begin{array}{r} 0.7 \\ \times\, 0.6 \\ \hline \end{array}$$ $$\begin{array}{r} 0.08 \\ \times\quad 3 \\ \hline \end{array}$$ $$\begin{array}{r} 0.05 \\ \times\, 0.9 \\ \hline \end{array}$$

Determine the quotient.

$0.7\overline{)2.8}$ $0.3\overline{)0.09}$ $0.8\overline{)24}$ $6\overline{)0.42}$

Determine the product.

$5\dfrac{1}{4} \times \dfrac{3}{8} =$ $\dfrac{4}{5} \times 7\dfrac{2}{3} =$ $3\dfrac{5}{7} \times \dfrac{4}{9} =$ $\dfrac{1}{2} \times 5\dfrac{2}{3} =$

Name _____ Date _____

Determine the product.

$$\begin{array}{r} 0.03 \\ \times\ \ 0.5 \\ \hline \end{array}$$

$$\begin{array}{r} 0.008 \\ \times\qquad 7 \\ \hline \end{array}$$

$$\begin{array}{r} 9 \\ \times\ 0.9 \\ \hline \end{array}$$

Determine the quotient.

$$0.03\overline{)2.1}$$

$$5\overline{)0.35}$$

$$4\overline{)3.2}$$

Determine the product.

$$3\frac{1}{3} \times \frac{7}{10} =$$

$$\frac{5}{8} \times 2\frac{3}{7} =$$

$$3\frac{3}{4} \times \frac{5}{6} =$$

Determine the area.

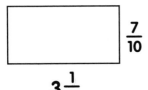

$$\frac{7}{10}$$

$$3\frac{1}{3}$$

$$1\frac{3}{4}$$

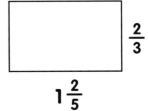

$$\frac{2}{3}$$

$$\frac{4}{5}$$

$$1\frac{2}{5}$$

_____ square units _____ square units _____ square units

Name _____ Date _____

Determine the product.

$$\begin{array}{r} 0.7 \\ \times\ 0.09 \\ \hline \end{array}$$

$$\begin{array}{r} 0.003 \\ \times\qquad 8 \\ \hline \end{array}$$

$$\begin{array}{r} 6 \\ \times\ 0.3 \\ \hline \end{array}$$

$$\begin{array}{r} 0.03 \\ \times\qquad 9 \\ \hline \end{array}$$

Determine the quotient.

$8\overline{)4.8}$

$0.7\overline{)0.14}$

$0.9\overline{)3.6}$

$0.05\overline{)0.45}$

Determine the product.

$8\dfrac{1}{3} \times \dfrac{5}{7} =$

$\dfrac{3}{5} \times 7\dfrac{1}{7} =$

$4\dfrac{3}{7} \times \dfrac{4}{5} =$

$\dfrac{2}{9} \times 5\dfrac{4}{7} =$

Determine the area.

$2\dfrac{2}{3}$ $5\dfrac{1}{2}$

$2\dfrac{1}{4}$ $2\dfrac{1}{4}$

$1\dfrac{1}{3}$ $3\dfrac{1}{8}$

$3\dfrac{1}{4}$ $2\dfrac{2}{3}$

_____ square units   _____ square units   _____ square units   _____ square units

Name _____ Date _____

Determine the quotient.

$0.4\overline{)1.2}$ $8\overline{)0.48}$ $7\overline{)4.2}$

Determine the product.

$5\frac{1}{4} \times \frac{3}{8} =$ $\frac{2}{3} \times 4\frac{1}{2} =$ $6\frac{1}{4} \times \frac{4}{7} =$

Determine the area.

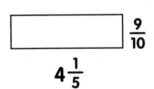
$4\frac{1}{5}$ $\frac{9}{10}$

_____ square units

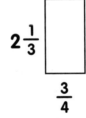
$2\frac{1}{3}$ $\frac{3}{4}$

_____ square units

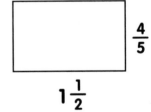
$1\frac{1}{2}$ $\frac{4}{5}$

_____ square units

Compare the expressions. Use <, >, or =.

$(3 + 4) \times (15 - 6)$ ◯ $(11 - 3) \times (5 + 3)$

$48 \div (15 - 7)$ ◯ $(53 - 4) \div (9 - 2)$

$45 \div (11 - 2)$ ◯ $(4 \times 8) \div (5 - 1)$

Name _____ **Date** _____

Determine the quotient.

$9\overline{)2.7}$ | $7\overline{)0.42}$ | $8\overline{)0.8}$ | $0.03\overline{)2.1}$

Determine the product.

$8\frac{1}{5} \times \frac{3}{7} =$ | $\frac{5}{6} \times 7\frac{2}{3} =$ | $5\frac{3}{4} \times \frac{3}{5} =$ | $\frac{5}{8} \times 4\frac{1}{4} =$

Determine the area.

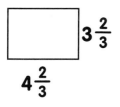 $3\frac{2}{3}$
$4\frac{2}{3}$

$2\frac{1}{3}$ ▢
$5\frac{1}{3}$

▢ $2\frac{3}{4}$
$4\frac{1}{2}$

▢ $3\frac{1}{3}$
$4\frac{3}{5}$

_____ square units | _____ square units | _____ square units | _____ square units

---

Compare the expressions. Use <, >, or =.

$(12 - 3) \times (24 \div 3) \bigcirc (30 + 6) \times (5 - 3)$ | $72 \div (11 - 2) \bigcirc (6 \times 8) \div (6 - 2)$

$17 \times (15 - 12) \bigcirc (45 + 7) \div (3 - 2)$ | $(35 + 13) \div 6 \bigcirc 2 \times (100 \div 25)$

71

Name _____ **Date** _____

Determine the product.

$2\frac{3}{4} \times \frac{5}{6} =$ $\frac{1}{9} \times 7\frac{3}{8} =$ $4\frac{1}{3} \times \frac{2}{5} =$

Determine the area.

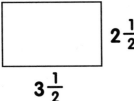
$2\frac{1}{2}$
$3\frac{1}{2}$

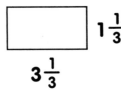
$1\frac{1}{3}$
$3\frac{1}{3}$

$3\frac{1}{4}$
$5\frac{1}{2}$

_____ square units   _____ square units   _____ square units

Compare the expressions. Use <, >, or =.

$7 \times (40 \div 10)$ ◯ $(24 - 17) \times 5$

$10 \times (3 + 5)$ ◯ $(4 + 5) \times (3 \times 3)$

$36 \div (6 - 2)$ ◯ $(7 \times 7) - 40$

Determine what fraction is missing from each equation.

$\frac{2}{3} \times$ ☐ $= \frac{14}{24}$ ☐ $\times \frac{2}{9} = \frac{6}{45}$ $\frac{7}{8} \times \frac{3}{4} =$

Name _____ **Date** _____

Determine the product.

$7\frac{1}{2} \times \frac{3}{4} =$ $\frac{2}{3} \times 5\frac{1}{5} =$ $2\frac{5}{7} \times \frac{3}{4} =$ $\frac{5}{9} \times 4\frac{3}{7} =$

Determine the area.

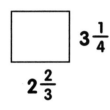 $3\frac{1}{4}$ 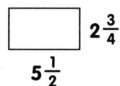 $2\frac{3}{4}$ 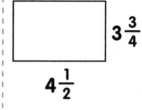 $3\frac{3}{4}$ 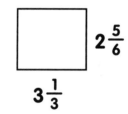 $2\frac{5}{6}$

$2\frac{2}{3}$ $5\frac{1}{2}$ $4\frac{1}{2}$ $3\frac{1}{3}$

_____ square units   _____ square units   _____ square units   _____ square units

---

Compare the expressions. Use <, >, or =.

$9 \times (20 - 16)$ ◯ $(4 + 3) \times 8$ $50 \div (7 - 2)$ ◯ $(6 - 1) \times 4$

$7 \times (4 + 5)$ ◯ $(8 - 2) \times (20 \div 5)$ $(13 + 22) \div 5$ ◯ $2 \times (100 - 98)$

Determine what fraction is missing from each equation.

$\frac{5}{7} \times = \frac{40}{63}$ $ \times \frac{6}{7} = \frac{42}{56}$ $\frac{4}{9} \times = \frac{8}{63}$ $ \times \frac{3}{8} = \frac{12}{72}$

Name _____ Date _____

Determine the area.

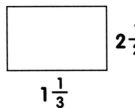 $2\frac{1}{2}$

$1\frac{1}{3}$

_____ square units

$1\frac{2}{3}$

$4\frac{1}{2}$

_____ square units

$3\frac{1}{4}$

$3\frac{1}{2}$

_____ square units

Compare the expressions. Use <, >, or =.

$$6 \times (4 + 3) \bigcirc 5 \times (4 + 4)$$

$$24 \div (3 + 3) \bigcirc 32 \div (4 + 4)$$

$$(5 + 3) \times 9 \bigcirc 80 - (24 \div 3)$$

Determine what fraction is missing from each equation.

$$\frac{2}{5} \times \underline{} = \frac{6}{20}$$

$$\frac{4}{5} \times \frac{3}{8} = \underline{}$$

$$\underline{} \times \frac{2}{9} = \frac{6}{63}$$

Write four related facts.

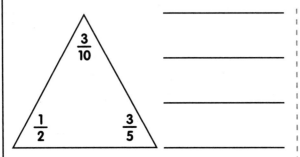

_____

_____

_____

_____

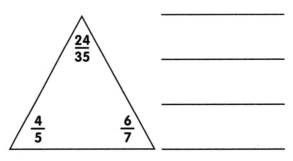

_____

_____

_____

_____

Name _____ **Date** _____

Determine the area.

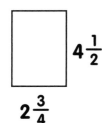 $4\frac{1}{2}$

$2\frac{3}{4}$

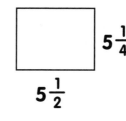 $2\frac{1}{3}$

$2\frac{5}{6}$

$5\frac{1}{4}$

$5\frac{1}{2}$

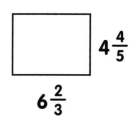 $4\frac{4}{5}$

$6\frac{2}{3}$

_____ square units   _____ square units   _____ square units   _____ square units

---

Compare the expressions. Use <, >, or =.

$20 \times (8 + 2)$ ◯ $(9 - 5) \times 50$ $(5 - 1) \times 25$ ◯ $18 + (9 \times 9)$

$7 \times (10 - 6)$ ◯ $15 + (8 \times 2)$ $36 \div (9 - 3)$ ◯ $36 \div (9 - 5)$

Determine what fraction is missing from each equation.

$\frac{3}{7} \times$ _____ $= \frac{12}{35}$ _____ $\times \frac{4}{5} = \frac{24}{35}$ $\frac{2}{5} \times \frac{5}{9} =$ $\frac{3}{4} \times \frac{7}{9} =$

Write four related facts.

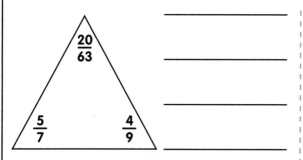 _____

_____

_____

_____

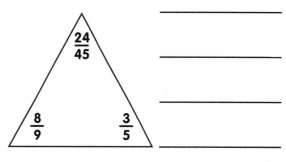 _____

_____

_____

_____

Name _____ **Date** _____

Compare the expressions. Use <, >, or =.

$$7 \times (3 + 4) \bigcirc 5 \times (5 + 5)$$

$$10 \times (3 + 7) \bigcirc 50 + (7 \times 7)$$

$$14 \times (10 - 7) \bigcirc 7 \times (10 - 4)$$

Determine what fraction is missing from each equation.

$$\frac{1}{2} \times \underline{\quad} = \frac{5}{16} \qquad \frac{3}{4} \times \underline{\quad} = \frac{21}{36} \qquad \frac{5}{6} \times \frac{3}{4} = \underline{\quad}$$

Write four related facts.

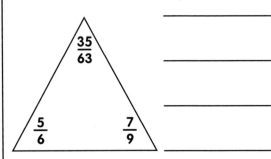

_____

_____

_____

_____

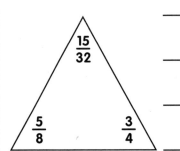

_____

_____

_____

_____

Write an equal expression using repeated addition.

$$\frac{2}{3} \times 4 = \qquad \frac{4}{9} \times 5 = \qquad \frac{1}{2} \times 6 =$$

Name _____ Date _____

Compare the expressions. Use <, >, or =.

75 – (8 × 4) ◯ 6 × (15 – 8)   (100 – 40) ÷ 10 ◯ 3 × (10 + 10)

22 + (5 × 9) ◯ 23 + (6 × 9)   63 ÷ (10 – 1) ◯ 90 – (9 ÷ 9)

Determine what fraction is missing from each equation.

$\dfrac{3}{8}$ ×   = $\dfrac{12}{40}$ × $\dfrac{7}{10}$ = $\dfrac{56}{90}$ $\dfrac{6}{8}$ × $\dfrac{7}{9}$ = $\dfrac{7}{8}$ ×   = $\dfrac{21}{56}$

Write four related facts.

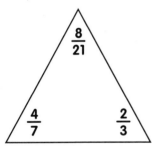

_____

_____

_____

_____

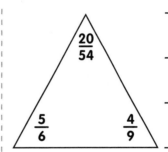

_____

_____

_____

_____

Write an equal expression using repeated addition.

$\dfrac{3}{4}$ × 7 = $\dfrac{5}{6}$ × 4 =

$\dfrac{1}{9}$ × 4 = $\dfrac{7}{9}$ × 6 =

Week 1-A

210	150	600
8 cubic units	16 cubic units	5 cubic units
50 + 2 + 0.7 + 0.06	4 + 0.2 + 0.09 + 0.003	800 + 10 + 9 + 0.6
35 is 7 times greater than 5. 35 is 5 times greater than 7.	48 is 6 times greater than 8. 48 is 8 times greater than 6.	133 is 7 times greater than 19. 133 is 19 times greater than 7.

Week 1-B

5,400	40,000	56,000	240,000
24 cubic units	20 cubic units	15 cubic units	20 cubic units
50 + 2 + 0.9 + 0.01 + 0.006	300 + 80 + 5 + 0.4 + 0.02	10 + 6 + 0.1 + 0.07 + 0.004	900 + 10 + 5 + 0.5 + 0.08
126 is 9 times greater than 14. 126 is 14 times greater than 9.	110 is 22 times greater than 5. 110 is 5 times greater than 22.	600 is 12 times greater than 50. 600 is 50 times greater than 12.	800 is 25 times greater than 32. 800 is 32 times greater than 25.

Week 2-A

6 cubic units	12 cubic units	8 cubic units
9 + 0.2 + 0.08 + 0.006	70 + 8 + 0.5 + 0.04	300 + 90 + 4 + 0.7 + 0.02
45 is 5 times greater than 9. 45 is 9 times greater than 5.	100 is 4 times greater than 25. 100 is 25 times greater than 4.	140 is 20 times greater than 7. 140 is 7 times greater than 20.
21	42	49

Week 2-B

12 cubic units	15 cubic units	14 cubic units	24 cubic units
50 + 2 + 0.9 + 0.03 + 0.008	10 + 7 + 0.6 + 0.08 + 0.008	2,000 + 500 + 60 + 9 + 0.7	400 + 80 + 2 + 0.6 + 0.05 + 0.009
238 is 17 times greater than 14. 238 is 14 times greater than 17.	891 is 3 times greater than 297. 891 is 297 times greater than 3.	2,090 is 55 times greater than 38. 2,090 is 38 times greater than 55.	1,144 is 286 times greater than 4. 1,144 is 4 times greater than 286.
20	72	55	2

Week 3-A

6 + 0.2 + 0.05 + 0.004	30 + 8 + 0.2 + 0.09	100 + 80 + 6 + 0.4 + 0.07
270 is 90 times greater than 3. 270 is 3 times greater than 90.	180 is 15 times greater than 12. 180 is 12 times greater than 15.	864 is 36 times greater than 24. 864 is 24 times greater than 36.
27	21	9
12	6	7

Week 3-B

20 + 8 + 0.6 + 0.07 + 0.001	900 + 80 + 5 + 0.6 + 0.04	2,000 + 300 + 50 + 8 + 0.2 + 0.06	50 + 9 + 0.7 + 0.03 + 0.007
3,500 is 50 times greater than 70. 3,500 is 70 times greater than 50.	1,014 is 26 times greater than 39. 1,014 is 39 times greater than 26.	5,561 is 83 times greater than 67. 5,561 is 67 times greater than 83.	3,843 is 7 times greater than 549. 3,843 is 549 times greater than 7.
56	51	9	56
7	4	120	7

Week 4-A

120 is 8 times greater than 15. 120 is 15 times greater than 8.	1,000 is 25 times greater than 40. 1,000 is 40 times greater than 25.	330 is 22 times greater than 15. 330 is 15 times greater than 22.
8	20	28
48	5	6
100 times greater	1,000 times smaller	1,000 times smaller

Week 4-B

988 is 26 times greater than 38. 988 is 38 times greater than 26.	3,825 is 9 times greater than 425. 3,825 is 425 times greater than 9.	221 is 17 times greater than 13. 221 is 13 times greater than 17.	3,060 is 68 times greater than 45. 3,060 is 45 times greater than 68.
9	48	42	8
162	1	2	50
1,000 times smaller	1,000 times smaller	10,000 times greater	100,000 times smaller

Week 5-A

18	56	28
6	72	43
100 times smaller	1,000 times greater	100 times smaller
12 cubic units	8 cubic units	12 cubic units

Week 5-B

42	54	90	3
9	42	154	180
10,000 times greater	100 times smaller	10,000 times smaller	100 times greater
18 cubic units	16 cubic units	27 cubic units	24 cubic units

Week 6-A

56	900	72
100 times smaller	10 times greater	10,000 times smaller
12 cubic units	20 cubic units	24 cubic units
13/4	17/6	17/2

Week 6-B

479	5,000	350	1,200
100,000 times greater	1,000 times smaller	10,000 times smaller	100,000 times greater
24 cubic units	40 cubic units	48 cubic units	36 cubic units
61/8	62/7	65/6	59/9

Week 7-A

100 times smaller	1,000 times greater	10,000 times greater
30 cubic units	40 cubic units	24 cubic units
19/4	26/9	26/5
3 3/4	3 1/5	2 5/6

Week 7-B

100,000 times smaller	10,000 times greater	10,000 times greater	100,000 times greater
60 cubic units	64 cubic units	48 cubic units	36 cubic units
47/6	77/9	56/9	75/8
8 2/6	6 3/7	9 2/9	8 4/7

Week 8-A

18 cubic units	32 cubic units	36 cubic units
27/5	32/3	17/2
4 1/2	4 1/4	4 4/7
3.8	5.24	586.5

Week 8-B

60 cubic units	64 cubic units	45 cubic units	36 cubic units
59/6	44/5	62/8	68/7
7 6/7	7 5/8	8 3/5	8 8/9
45.27	33.608	59.3	62.96

Week 9-A

31/4	49/8	86/9
8 2/3	9 4/5	9 3/8
681.7	18	253.79
7/9	7/10	15/21

Week 9-B

68/7	71/8	53/7	58/9
9 5/9	9 1/4	7 2/3	9 3/4
216	38.257	52.78	16.3
61/70	31/36	33/40	13/21

Week 10-A

8 3/4	3 2/7	8 4/5
52.7	4	218.45
9/10	7/12	13/15
10,000	10^2	1,000

Week 10-B

8 6/7	9 5/6	6 1/8	5 7/9
785.5	25	6.29	2.316
53/56	34/40	7/14	41/45
100,000	10^3	100	10^6

Week 11-A

6.281	2.9	542
5/8	11/20	13/18
1,000	10^2	10,000
10^5	10^8	10^5

Week 11-B

15.298	32.6	28	52.65
62/63	67/90	7/16	37/40
100,000	10^4	1,000,000	10^2
10^5	10^6	10^8	10^9

Answer Key

Week 12-A

7/9	19/28	8/10
1,000,000	10^3	100
10^9	10^4	10^2
0.32 + 0.13 = 0.45	0.07 + 0.46 = 0.53	0.51 + 0.25 = 0.76

Week 12-B

17/21	31/36	24/25	19/20
100,000	10^2	1,000	10^4
10^6	10^5	10^{13}	10^7
0.23 + 0.23 = 0.46	0.47 + 0.14 = 0.61	0.14 + 0.43 = 0.57	0.31 + 0.18 = 0.49

Week 13-A

100	10^4	100,000
10^9	10^{15}	10^6
0.17 + 0.24 = 0.41	0.52 + 0.29 = 0.81	0.04 + 0.09 = 0.13
16	32	+ 5, × 2

Week 13-B

10,000,000	10^6	100,000,000	10^4
10^{14}	10^2	10^7	10^5
0.37 + 0.19 = 0.56	0.51 + 0.17 = 0.68	0.04 + 0.03 = 0.07	0.23 + 0.38 = 0.61
35	73	× 3, + 7, − 4	

Week 14-A

10^5	10^{11}	10^{10}
0.24 + 0.18 = 0.42	0.28 + 0.25 = 0.53	0.09 + 0.36 = 0.45
7	27	÷ 4, × 6
1/10	5/9	1/4

Week 14-B

10^7	10^3	10^4	10^{12}
0.62 + 0.09 = 0.71	0.27 + 0.18 = 0.45	0.32 + 0.32 = 0.64	0.16 + 0.30 = 0.46
30	63	× 9, ÷ 3, + 19	
5/18	5/8	17/40	11/20

Week 15-A

0.18 + 0.12 = 0.3	0.42 + 0.24 = 0.66	0.16 + 0.28 = 0.44
42	8	+6, ÷3
3/8	1/12	17/30
12	10	28

Week 15-B

0.49 + 0.13 = 0.62	0.4 + 0.12 = 0.52	0.57 + 0.19 = 0.76	0.28 + 0.27 = 0.55
105	119	÷ 9, + 19, + 27	
1/21	5/18	13/24	25/90
56	54	42	36

Week 16-A

30	100	+ 16, × 3
3/10	5/12	2/15
40	27	20
27.98	90.92	41.3

Week 16-B

34	15	÷ 4, + 23, × 4	
8/21	7/24	31/63	5/18
96	30	60	54
28.44	303.37	82.64	64.66

Week 17-A

7/15	12/32	6/16
49	20	24
26.33	114.32	66.63
48 cubic m	90 cubic cm	56 cubic in.

Week 17-B

13/18	10/63	5/24	9/56
48	72	42	32
38.768	320.24	631.974	59.13
70 cubic m	900 cubic cm	120 cubic in.	63 cubic ft

Week 18-A

10	12	35
81.12	634.218	231.5
63 cubic ft	90 cubic cm	54 cubic m
36	8	1

Week 18-B

56	60	72	42
331.214	616.68	62.24	55.375
150 cubic ft	72 cubic cm	98 cubic m	180 cubic in.
63	31	11	4

Week 19-A

60.182	892.84	175.483
45 cubic ft	24 cubic in.	40 cubic km
8	5	90
0.37 − 0.06 = 0.31	0.25 − 0.03 = 0.22	0.49 − 0.07 = 0.42

Week 19-B

34.423	544.347	676.018	555.87
48 cubic ft	90 cubic in.	72 cubic km	120 cubic m
3	39	37	4
0.63 − 0.07 = 0.56	0.87 − 0.48 = 0.39	0.36 − 0.05 = 0.31	0.54 − 0.16 = 0.38

Week 20-A

40 cubic m	63 cubic cm	105 cubic ft
48	8	48
0.31 − 0.04 = 0.27	0.25 − 0.13 = 0.12	0.42 − 0.15 = 0.27
1/12	1/20	1/18

Week 20-B

168 cubic m	504 cubic cm	192 cubic ft	135 cubic in.
7	19	2	21
0.94 − 0.59 = 0.35	0.57 − 0.03 = 0.54	0.51 − 0.24 = 0.27	0.36 − 0.18 = 0.18
1/36	1/42	1/24	1/45

Week 21-A

5	3	31
0.39 − 0.15 = 0.24	0.52 − 0.03 = 0.49	0.17 − 0.09 = 0.08
1/14	1/10	1/24
A(4,7) B(5,2) C(7,3)	A(1,5) B(9,9) C(10,3)	A(1,9) B(7,1) C(9,10)

Week 21-B

8	4	3	10
0.73 − 0.27 = 0.46	0.34 − 0.03 = 0.31	0.52 − 0.15 = 0.37	0.94 − 0.35 = 0.59
1/81	1/40	1/56	1/60
A(1,6) B(7,2) C(9,6)	A(1,1) B(7,3) C(10,6)	A(4,7) B(9,3) C(10,10)	A(0,5) B(4,3) C(9,0)

Week 22-A

0.23 − 0.06 = 0.17	0.58 − 0.35 = 0.23	0.73 − 0.27 = 0.46
1/20	1/21	1/18
A(4,3) B(5,9) C(10,4)	A(2,8) B(9,8) C(9,4)	A(4,2) B(7,8) C(10,0)
16.9	17.83	12.46

Week 22-B

0.27 − 0.06 = 0.21	0.43 − 0.37 = 0.06	0.84 − 0.16 = 0.68	0.61 − 0.24 = 0.37
1/54	1/56	1/49	1/48
A(1,7) B(6,8) C(8,2)	A(4,6) B(8,10) C(10,6)	A(3,6) B(5,0) C(8,3)	A(2,4) B(5,7) C(8,4)
37.8	56.13	86.2	5.91

Week 23-A

1/4	1/24	1/24
A(1,9) B(5,4) C(6,1)	A(4,10) B(7,2) C(9,0)	A(3,0) B(6,1) C(9,7)
80.5	64.79	83.11
8	14	9

Week 23-B

1/40	1/64	1/28	1/27
A(3,2) B(5,5) C(9,3)	A(3,1) B(5,2) C(7,3)	A(2,7) B(6,6) C(10,1)	A(3,7) B(8,4) C(9,9)
25.74	7.92	45.22	66.79
24	20	24	15

Week 24-A

A(2,8) B(6,1) C(7,7)	A(4,8) B(6,7) C(8,6)	A(2,4) B(7,7) C(7,4)
12.9	7.43	47.7
10	12	10
1,376	1,428	1,472

Week 24-B

A(3,4) B(6,0) C(10,7)	A(2,5) B(3,4) C(4,3)	A(2,9) B(4,4) C(8,3)	A(2,3) B(4,7) C(8,1)
36.47	16.31	17.37	133.7
13	22	32	25
4,644	4,134	4,384	15,747

Week 25-A

57.17	56.3	19.6
16	16	14
864	944	1,995
700	60	45

Week 25-B

72.75	25.14	127.5	41.01
20	60	36	36
5,626	5,395	4,288	21,675
900	96	69	504

Week 26-A

18	18	11
1,537	3,355	2,976
68	14,080	364
<	<	=

Week 26-B

17	24	30	20
4,644	7,252	15,392	75,888
116	15,840	2,268	42,240
>	>	<	>

Week 27-A

720	4,316	2,368
19,000	276	219
<	<	<
4/15	7/24	6/25

Week 27-B

3,492	1,332	19,312	49,551
73,000	6,804	654	2,016
>	<	<	>
21/72	35/63	9/16	12/63

Week 28-A

1,020	14,080	315
>	<	<
12/35	10/18	14/30
0.24	5.6	2.1

Week 28-B

384	12,320	1,505	84,480
<	<	>	<
48/63	28/45	14/56	30/42
0.028	0.18	0.045	0.49

Week 29-A

<	<	>
16/35	6/35	10/24
3.2	0.28	0.012
0.8	0.9	3

Week 29-B

<	<	>	>
8/63	24/35	56/72	6/20
0.21	0.006	0.63	4.5
0.6	9	80	0.7

Week 30-A

3/40	9/16	7/16
0.32	4.5	0.027
0.6	0.6	3
11/8	14/6	26/21

Week 30-B

36/49	15/48	35/54	28/40
0.63	0.42	0.24	0.045
4	0.3	30	0.07
63/32	92/15	104/63	17/6

Week 31-A

0.015	0.056	8.1
70	0.07	0.8
70/30	85/56	75/24
70/30	28/20	14/15

Week 31-B

0.063	0.024	1.8	0.27
0.6	0.2	4	9
125/21	150/35	124/35	78/63
88/6	81/16	100/24	104/12

Week 32-A

3	0.06	0.6
63/32	18/6	100/28
189/50	21/12	12/10
<	<	<

Week 32-B

0.3	0.06	0.1	70
123/35	115/18	69/20	85/32
154/9	112/9	99/8	230/15
=	<	<	=

Week 33-A

55/24	59/72	26/15
35/4	40/9	143/8
<	<	=
7/8	3/5	21/32

Week 33-B

45/8	52/15	57/28	155/63
104/12	121/8	135/8	170/18
<	>	<	>
8/9	7/8	2/7	4/9

Week 34-A

20/6	45/6	91/8
>	=	=
3/4	12/40	3/7

$1/2 \times 3/5 = 3/10$	$4/5 \times 6/7 = 24/35$
$3/5 \times 1/2 = 3/10$	$6/7 \times 4/5 = 24/35$
$3/10 \div 1/2 = 3/5$	$24/35 \div 4/5 = 6/7$
$3/10 \div 3/5 = 1/2$	$24/35 \div 6/7 = 4/5$

Week 34-B

99/8	119/18	231/8	480/15
=	<	>	<
4/5	6/7	10/45	21/36

$5/7 \times 4/9 = 20/63$	$8/9 \times 3/5 = 24/45$
$4/9 \times 5/7 = 20/63$	$3/5 \times 8/9 = 24/45$
$20/63 \div 5/7 = 4/9$	$24/45 \div 8/9 = 3/5$
$20/63 \div 4/9 = 5/7$	$24/45 \div 3/5 = 8/9$

Week 35-A

<	>	=
5/8	7/9	15/24

$5/7 \times 7/9 = 35/63$	$5/8 \times 3/4 = 15/32$	
$7/9 \times 5/7 = 35/63$	$3/4 \times 5/8 = 15/32$	
$35/63 \div 5/7 = 7/9$	$15/32 \div 5/8 = 3/4$	
$35/63 \div 7/9 = 5/7$	$15/32 \div 3/4 = 5/8$	
2/3 + 2/3 + 2/3 + 2/3	4/9 + 4/9 + 4/9 + 4/9 + 4/9	1/2 +1/2 + 1/2 + 1/2 + 1/2 + 1/2

Week 35-B

>	<	<	<
4/5	8/9	42/72	3/7

$4/7 \times 2/3 = 8/21$	$5/6 \times 4/9 = 20/54$		
$2/3 \times 4/7 = 8/21$	$4/9 \times 5/6 = 20/54$		
$8/21 \div 4/7 = 2/3$	$20/54 \div 5/6 = 4/9$		
$8/21 \div 2/3 = 4/7$	$20/54 \div 4/9 = 5/6$		
3/4 + 3/4 + 3/4 + 3/4 + 3/4 + 3/4 + 3/4	1/9 + 1/9 + 1/9 + 1/9	5/6 + 5/6 + 5/6 + 5/6	7/9 + 7/9 + 7/9 + 7/9 + 7/9 + 7/9